PIANO Praise & Worship

Volume #2

Creative Piano Settings by FRED BOCK

TABLE OF CONTENTS

All of these selections are brand new arrangements by Fred Bock and do not appear in any other piano collection. Might we suggest you take a look at *Piano Praise & Worship #1* (BG0749), containing 15 additional Praise & Worship arrangements by Fred Bock.

Fred Bock Music Company

THIS IS THE DAY

Les Garrett
Arranged by Fred Bock

mf
(echo)
mp
simile
mf
(echo)
mp
mf
mf
like a fanfare
f
3
mf legato

(echo)
mp
mf
(echo)
mp
mf
scherzo-like
no pedal!
f
l.h.
legato
mf
legato
f
OK to pedal now!
mf
f
8va
ff
l.h.
(ff)
r.h.

JESUS, NAME ABOVE ALL NAMES

Naida Hearn
Arranged by Fred Bock

In a flowing style (♩. = 58)

"Jesu, Joy of Man's Desiring"
Music by J.S. Bach

a tempo
a tempo
(rit. 2x)
(optional repeat)
ten. ten. ten.
ten. ten. ten.
mp

LORD, BE GLORIFIED/SANCTUARY

Bob Kilpatrick
John Thompson & Randy Scruggs
Arranged by Fred Bock

rit.
mf

f
mf
With a Gospel feel (♩ = 72)
f
"Sanctuary"
f
light rhythm

Stronger, more driving
f
suddenly
slowing
mf
(♩ = 60)
ten.
mp
mf
ten.
mp
8va
pp
pp
8ba

ALL HAIL, KING JESUS

Dave Moody
Arranged by Fred Bock

f
f
mf
3
melody legato
ten.
3
f

allargando
ff
slight accellerando
f
ff broaden
ff
grandioso
r.h.
l.h.
both hands 8va
fff

PRAISE THE NAME OF JESUS

Roy Hicks, Jr.
Arranged by Fred Bock

Gently, not too fast (♩ = 84)

mf
bring out l.h. melody
mp
mf
mf
f
mp
mf
mf

mf
Stately
mf
f
gradual rit.
mf
p

AWESOME GOD/I EXALT THEE

Richard Mullins
Pete Sanchez, Jr.
Arranged by Fred Bock

* play with side of thumb.

mf

rit.
mp
pp

OPEN OUR EYES

Bob Cull
Arranged by Fred Bock

ppp
let fade away

AS THE DEER

Martin Nystrom
Arranged by Fred Bock

a tempo
p
mp
mf
f
mp
mp
mf
f

strongly
slight
rit.
mf
l.h.
f
mf
mp
mp
r.h.
p

EMMANUEL

Bob McGee
Arranged by Fred Bock

With awe and mystery (𝅗𝅥 = 60)

* "O Come, O Come, Emmanuel"
Traditional Plainsong Chant

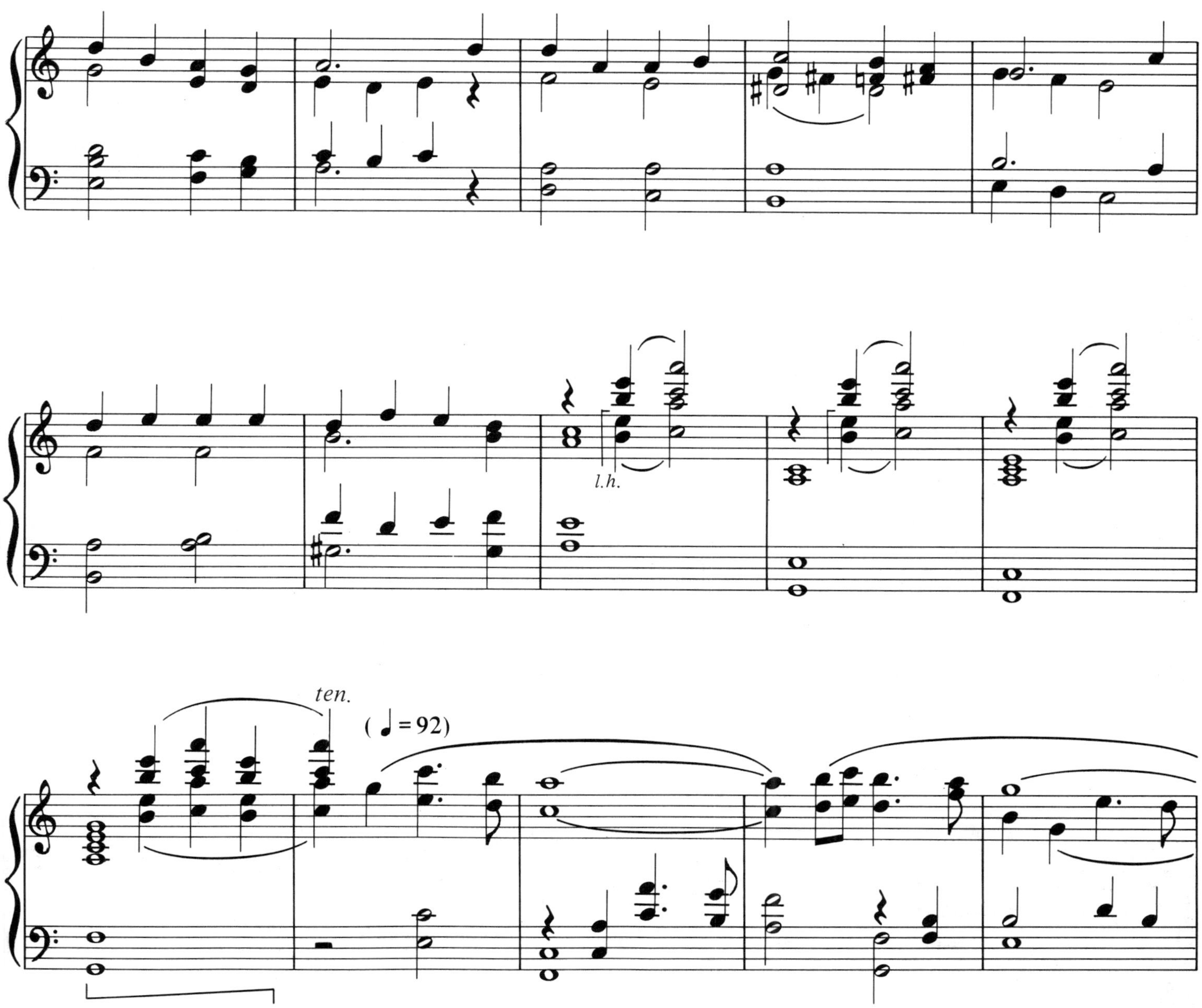

l.h.
l.h.
both hands 8va

HE HAS MADE ME GLAD

Leona Von Brethorst
Arranged by Fred Bock

f
8va

8va
8va
8va
f
ff
no ritard!
mf
both hands 8va
ff
mf

SHINE, JESUS, SHINE

Graham Kendrick
Arranged by Fred Bock

slight rit.
a tempo
legato
a tempo

mf
f
mf
both hands 8va
loco
(like a harp)
mf rit.
f
ten.
sub. mp
ten.
warm and legato

sub.
rit.
a tempo
(like the beginning)
8va
ten.
a tempo
loco
8va
slight rit.
8va
ten.

I WILL CALL UPON THE LORD

Michael O'Shields
Arranged by Fred Bock

f
mf
f
mf

f
mf
(♯)
8va
l.h.
8ba